To the memory of
Ben Fisher
Barbara Venables Fisher

ACKNOWLEDGEMENTS

I thank the Authors' Foundation for its support during the making of this collection.

Some of the poems have appeared in *The Guardian*, *The North* and *Stand*. 'Hole, Horse and Hellbox' is the text of Ronald King's artwork 'Tabernacle', published by Circle Press.

CONTENTS

The Afterlife

I've lived within half a mile of it
for twenty years. West
by the black iron weather-hen
half-strangled with clematis
on the garage roof
I can locate it. Past a low ridge
in the cliff face of a limestone dale
there's a cave in the bushes.

When the old tigers
were long since gone, leaving their
teeth, the valley people
would climb there with the dead
they thought most useful;

push them well in,

take them out again,
walk them around:
'They're coming! They're coming!'

> *We Malagasies love*
> *our second burials.*
> *We hire a band that comes*
> *in a van. Again*
> *with liquefaction almost done*
> *we hold our cherished ones*

in our arms. From the grave-clothes
they fall in gobbets as dog-food
falls from the can. We wrap them
in fresh dry linen. They
bless our lives with their happiness.

Walk them around the valley. Drop
here a finger
for the god that is a rat or a raven,
here a metatarsal
to set under the hearth for luck.

And what was luck?

The afterlife back then
was fairly long:
nothing demented like for ever,

nothing military. The afterlife
would come to the party.

On Spare Land

Wormwood
rank grass
kids' dens: the entire
little essay.

Commons without commoners
the Unadopted. A footpath worn
from corner to corner. Wormwood.

And how at the edge the hoardings
paralyse words high up
in the common air.

John Cage
on a bland enough midwestern
campus:
  – use random means
to set coordinates then
hang around at the intersection
all day if need be. There'll
be something to interest you!

Somewhere along the Pool

I like my long shapes, so that I can 'move', so that one half or part reacts against, while furthering the purpose of, the other.
IVON HITCHENS, 1960

This sump of light
draining from no seen source
walk dry no further
in a confident sulk
that draws the eye in
from under the entire weight at my back
of the City Art Gallery: no vista, no
viewpoint. But what's been shown
shifts, is gnomic
from whatever place along the pool
at one time or another
compels the mind, the unity bargaining
for more than one life.

Inner Voice

Getting old,
living alone, I still
talk too much but to myself.
I talk my way through
procedures like
carrying books downstairs.

The monologue's so stupid
I do it in farting Mockney
or worse, mincing
Estuarian: none of it worth
the touch of my own Standard Midland.

On the Wellingtonias at Pilleth

In a long canoe sunk to the gunwales
to dance on a board
as on the choppy water. The tall
sea-eagle in feathered trousers and the raven
plumed arm-wings waving, beaks agape;
salmon and bear stamping
saw-teeth snapping at the sky,
all with heads thrown back, wild eyes
taking in nothing. Four gods making
common cause at the people.
                              Moreover
beings of what seemed flesh
would lately float on gables or range themselves
on a wall, supported by *chi* in the clear
air under them that showed
the hillside beyond it. Their burning
gaze to rain down still while they faded.

Driving down off Axe Edge on the hot afternoon of the day
that would end with the full moon hung on the horizon at
twice its size, rounding a familiar bend then both of us
seeing differently the anomaly ahead, tall brown figure in a
limestone landscape. Reared on a crag to command the
desolate stock-car track, the quarry and the valley of the
Dove. Eyeless, dynamic, brutal, maybe a public sculpture
giant in rusted sheet metal, another expensive mistake. Pass
by the threat and it goes back nearer Nature: the three old

horses that always amble in the boggy roadside fields have criss-crossed the bluff, growing bigger all the while. They've arranged themselves on the naked steps of the summit and stand there asleep as a single conjoined thing against the sky waiting for the enormous moon to land and take them up.

Stone horn-shapes above
a peaceful enough gateway
and in the High Great Chamber
a plaster frieze where beasts and tall women
walk by among the trees
in the woodland above it all.

                    There are
parts of kings, brown old thigh-bones,
shin-bones, jaws, promiscuous teeth
packed out of reach in their own air
on high stone rails
ready in their chests to travel.

                    Odours
of shellfish and salmon rising from marble
counters in the pomp of the market
defer to the palms ranged above. Masque
in the Aquarium tank breasting the view
floor up to roof where the skirts
swish through the murk and sharks
ride up and pass

'Sunday 6.30 Rev. Handel Broadbent
IF I BE LIFTED UP'

Indeed. If so he be. The phut and fall
of a late firework.
                         Where the Lugg
between its alders wriggles and winds
fed once for a season or two with the leached-out
seepage driven down by the rain
out of hundreds of corpses, some
where Pilleth's ghostly church
squats on the dead, others across
the cropped slope of Bryn Glâs, buffered now
with alien fir.

                    The four Wellingtonias
planted low down, late and pictorially
as if hoping to settle the matter
stretching their single dark plumes towards the ridge
stopper the sightline along the valley
and make us a view.

On Hearing I'd Outlived My Son the Linguist

Two days since I heard you were gone
suddenly in your forties and me still not quite eighty

and hour by hour today with no whole word all
the emptied patterns of your talk come crowding
into my brain for shelter:
bustling, warm, exact. You'd be interested.

Little Jazz

(for John Lucas)

Trumpet-players, all too often
beset by narcissism, heroism
leadership, hypochondria
the flourish, the pain of it all,
call for our understanding
and deserve it.

But the plucky one had to be
Eldridge. Even when no sound came out
you could still tell what he meant.

Target

Ken Smith
woke out of weeks of coma
aphasic. He muttered
they guessed. He gestured
they scribbled. He nodded
or not. One day the old exasperation
won through. Wearily: 'What's
the word for CHAIR?'

Jumping the Gun

Vivaldi fell into the Circle of Fifths
(banjo chords on request)
because it was there

– rather prematurely some might think.

Impurities

With speckled breast
shoulders and back and
with freckled brow –Look!

that Roman canting –
fine for getting about
if you feel you have to
if you know you must –

wash beforehand
wash after wash
between times all the while
with wood water
clean off its head with desires

mottled hand at work

no need to be told. Always
known I lied
whether I spoke or not. Even the dreams
once true within their codes
dislodge. Not a problem.
a flung curse

fashion of being cursed

a hangman washes down his dead.
tug the noose open and the last
inbreath trapped in the carcass
belches and blurts out loud by the lips
with a great stench to work on through
washing

then old air on its way
out across town with rare news
gathered in the dark while that body
dismantles itself all around, neons
riding-lights, failed
sperms jerking with broken tails
snapping out spastic

hospital heroin
quietens breathing
right down to where it
empties then not refills. The last
breath is outwards. No more.

on mottled underwings

paired outlines in a picture
a vase a shed
an unused galvanised bucket
and a nipple, maybe visited,
by art suspended
against the moment when one
stains the other

in the warm hospital
men lie tidy, half-naked
wired up, tubed up, listless
ticking, beeping

in the warm hospital

False Winds

With false winds
hung off the walls and the vane
baffled, all's well
for an hour, for a day.

Sanctuary

The fox, from nowhere,
springs to the roof of the empty kennel
and stands there, grubby. At which
a staring cock pheasant shoots straight up behind
and to either side symmetrically
a pair of magpies go tumbling up.

Fox slopes off along a wall; the pheasant hen
with unbroken concentration softly
ripples her patterned feathers
on the gravel below. The season already took
the hundreds of nesting bumble-bees
whose sanctuary this has been, and they're
nowhere. Not a bee-husk to be seen.

Syntax

March. The cat
with eyes askew
rubs her great head hard
against the last stalk of kale
left standing in the mud
till it breaks
and the green juice gleams.

Plot

Beyond the desperate leeks
and the failing celeriac
the row of Jerusalem artichokes
rocks every way in the gale
while the tubers
huddle below in their word-nest.
Squat. Knobbled. Complacent.
Carminative. Of indescribable flavour.

A Damp Night

'It's been a damp night' I hear myself say
walking out into the yard alone
and every imaginable idea
falls into line behind that lead.

It's as well to check the observation
in case the lead's deluded. Check.

It's been a damp night.

The Skyline in the Wall Mirror

Cold, and half a mile off behind me
the skyline in the wall mirror,
pasture when last looked at,
juts dark, its dip and sag
as good as lamp-black
and the right not to know what it's made of
revives. I guess clinker
cinders and slag: dense, dead
unstable. I always
had cinders ready. I have ashes.

Dancing Neanderthal

Stronger muscles than ours;
sharper tools –

Could speak?

Possibly.

Write?

Didn't. Unless with sharp stones
they incised their skins
that would die with them, observing
the ban on lasting records.

Traffic in symbols? Paint on rocks?

Couldn't?

Didn't. May have been foresight and hard taboo
to stop themselves inventing
religion, football or flags. Our world's ways of life
keep strong by prohibitions; and they may just have been
better than us at that, as they no doubt were
at contemplating extinction.

They could have danced?

All night, with that much muscle.

Sung?

No reason why not.

Hard wired to diatonic?

At Brough-on-Noe

What's good
is the way there seem to be
more waters than there are, poured
out of the rows of hills
to the valley bottom. There seem
to be more side lanes and alleys
that there ever were. What feels
like a village is no more than a road junction
mounted on a wandering confluence
and twisted to fit.

And the mismatch
chops up appearances
so that each part, each house,
row of trees, block of viewless
buildings marked grey on the map
as 'works' settled askew,
has to announce itself
as newly created. It moves
and stays put. There's
no single place to be
at Brough.

'Adjectives': the Novel; the Movie

Basil Bunting: 'Adjectives drain nouns'

Defending more than defensive. Ill-equipped, formal,
    luxurious. Defending.

Generous, invasive, status-conscious. Anxious, generous.

Shallow, acquisitive, kitted out, entertaining.

Ill-tended, ill-fed, worn: stale tending to foul.

Grimy, well-organised, obvious. Drunk.

Questing, Attentive. Reserved. Contained

Shocking Pink

(for Glyn Hughes)

Moving for a spell and in a mood
to a gritstone moor conserved
with care to be disquieting

and making in my sodden acid
square walled out of blanket bog
a compost heap – what else? –
so as to feel at home

I set it in the lee of the wall against
stones of tobacco-brown
blackened with lichen, all
good and grim. My mood,
my garden: outline and ooze.

So much for style. At spreading-time,
shame. The lichen-loving
compost bugs unweathered the wall
to what, exposed in the shadows,
looked like an abandoned headboard
dumped from a double bed, quilted
in a coy shade of salmon
paste: interior *chic*. No hope of hiding it
from visitors from town. No point any longer
in making them sleep in horse blankets.

Long Ago in a Town in the Provinces

At a poetry party,
having taken a shine to my conversation
or possibly my art, led me
to find her husband, talking in his corner.
'You *must* meet Roy! He's
emphatically OK.'
                              'I wish
that just once in a while
you'd collect somebody who *wasn't*
OK at all. Somebody shifty,
visibly devious, with unwholesome
views. Possibly quite interesting.
Hello Roy.'

Travel

Taking a detour past the police cordon
wondering how it was that not a single
spectator had turned out for the public hangings
all year: *Too schematic*,
said the young taxi-driver, *too formulaic*.

Log

*(designed to be inscribed on an inner surface of a
trunk cut lengthwise into planks then reassembled
as a standing sculpture: a log book)*

oh
        horns
rear and
        tower and
twig out and
        lopped
cower and
        tangle

split all and
        Myrddin Emrys
trapped for an age
        just now
slipped out again

Of the Qualities

1 *Petulant*

Somebody said Pissarro
set himself problems he'd solved already.

Somebody else
said the same about Duke Ellington.

They want their money back.

2 *Importunate*

Often when I seat myself in this armchair
with my thoughts and my notebook
the cat wades carefully along the tops of the furniture,
takes up a blocking position between
my face and my book
and just stands there purring and staring
as if by right. And possibly so.

Quite possibly I love the old cat
more than I love my thoughts. A private matter.

3 *Definitive*

'Presence. Unerring swing. Sober melancholy.'

– a passing remark on the constants in Louis Armstrong.

The third of these.

Hole, Horse and Hellbox: the Tabernacle Poems

Hole

FROM THE BOOK OF KINGS THEIR TRADES AND STATIONS

Wido King having brought forth THE MALE LINE, viz.

a pair of borough ratepayers and overseers of the poor

the younger of whom BEGAT

a ratepayer, overseer and churchwarden
and a ratepayer, overseer, schoolmaster, printer and overseer
of parish accounts

which schoolmaster and printer BEGAT

a Portreeve
a printer and a clothier

which clothier BEGAT

a shoemaker
a bookseller
a sergeant
and a bookbinder, printer, publisher, bookseller, author and
        Mayor

which author and Mayor BEGAT

a bookseller, printer, author, artist and Mayor
and a bookseller and printer

of whom the artist and Mayor BEGAT

a bookseller, printer, publisher and adventurer
and a bookseller, author and Mayor

which Mayor BEGAT, among others,

a printer, publisher and author

and which publisher and adventurer BEGAT

a banker in Brazil, who BEGAT

an artist, printer, publisher (&)

1

It's plain. The rule
and the example.
In from the world and all its directions
the rule must fall and there lie
shining alone. Any man
that sees this could make it for himself.
Any man. The example
fits to its rule and perfects it, once and then again.

Come on these letters late at night,
these unaccounted figures
lying together all ways up,
head down, backside to flank
they seem the demons they always were,
pushing themselves to tell
what is not, nor could ever be. Look –
these folk make mischief on their backs.

2

Word gets about. Gets about the town
wherever you can post it up. Cuts
flat, stamps flat, pads flat, stacks
and sells. Word lies down in rows then
stands up flat. Gets packed, travels
in pockets, in ledgers. In silence.
One thing turns out to be leading straight
to another.

3

But there's a force that starts to curve as it gathers and says
        MOVE
                War and energy. Peace with revolutions
                under the floorboards. Go looking.
Through countryside shaken out clean,
and everywhere fortunes falling out of it.
Shaken out clean, sewn up around houses lined with
mosaics in morocco. Gentlefolk learning their letters at last.
                Bargains in paper by the hundredweight.
Shift ground and settle. Rise. It may seem stable,

keeping a shop, but it's a circus all around, year after year,
with dynasties of every sort coming into fashion.
Sons in waiting, grandsons coming to the boil.

Horse

4

Firm on the rails, the rule
stamped softly home by example,
the mayoral robes passing from father
to son and back again, the more
valid if replicated, Q.E.D. All
the contracts of commerce reborn
and steadied, as the empire feels the current.
Steady as she goes, till everybody
reads print by force of law. Deviate,
develop – hardly.

5

Shifting so fast, at last there's one part
breaks loose and spins right off. Human
projectile, off balance, self-
driven into the thick of it,
thrashing through London as if it were America
on paper advances, quick dares. Well, then,
why not? Each one seemed a good idea
at the time. Side-swipes, head-ons,
baulked energies, tough forfeits. Riding
on the times, hard enough to send his genes
skidding halfway across the planet and back.

Riding on success, on work, on women; then
on nothing much at all. The deceased
showed signs of a prolonged series of blows
to the head with his own life. And he died,
knocked senseless in his own jailbait story,
the death of a publisher of fiction.

6

Over the curve of the planet and
out of earshot,
where the bang of the press
and the slug of the till never come.

Different money. Different papers.
Different feathers.

Hellbox

7

Borne, but not passively,
Behaving it out, whatever
Genial power ordained
The manner of the rule.

In Barnes, in Ironbridge, magnetic
attractions to sleeping books;
tremors of rightness tingling the scalp
in Tabernacle Street with more than
one man's purpose.

Peeling

(for b.v.f.)

First, she makes automatic writings for me
not in the manner of George Yeats
opening her legs to the hosts of the air:
more with a decent sidelong curiosity. Not
a readable word anywhere in it.

So to random choice, which can't be
mine: my *random* already corrupt
as language itself. So to *The Times*,
a light trance and a pin. Chance
wishes to say *The Glasgow*
Depot at Gushetfaulds/ 'Neighbours,
We'll not part tonight!'/ on our way
up the Nile to the first cataract/
the entertainment of war/ short growths
known as dards/ magic was once/ why
they stopped singing

some of which talk to me in a plainer
language than I'd been bargaining for

for starters.

A Masque of Resistances: Dancing in Chains

Tongue out, a woman's unruly member. Behind out,
everything out. Sprouting brazen hair-plumes from a circlet;
eyes that stare but won't take in, aggressive but not
predatory. Reddish clay, dung of a carnivore. Head up, both
arms banged down on a staff. Leader, leader.

Leading poverty that needn't beg. Little food needed to
keep thin pale arms at the ready. Lean back and laugh, let
the shoulder-bones show the strain. On the right day let the
steady poor loose against whatever enemy there is.

Free to sing out though silent for now. Band level across the
symmetrical brow, straight eyes darting side to side,
pretending conspiracy, planning pounces.

Lids lowered, still cheeks, arm raised to the back of
another's shoulder to clear a concentration downward to the
shackle. These are the Slaves' Games.

And this last one could be a help: looking out agreeably
unhampered, bitten away with action so far.

The Run to Brough

As if it might still be perilous
to leave the limestone cap and go
gradually into the other holding,
the other stone, the road
unhitches itself by an offset crossing
from the stark highway on the rise
and slips down into a dishevelled
basin of land and ragged purposes
with to one side shale slipped off the cliffs
and grassed over and to the other
villages sealed out of sight
under the ridge. Swing and
follow the waters down into the gullet
where the cut gorge sides hang trees
against the sky, the ground changes at the Grey Ditch

and out into Bradwell, mineral village, not old,
clambering over itself up the hillsides
at all angles, a medieval town with
every house a message. The run
to Brough goes straighter than the river,
slurry lagoons in the woods
and the disquiets left behind
or accumulated
for what Brough can do with them
or for anybody.

Stops and Stations

Another absolute black with pinholes picked in it as is the way with absolutes. Bright beads magnify what light there is. The dark deep with respect.

High over the little town and the railway in its cement cutting, a vacant institution among trees. Has been a small hospital, will be again: a certain swank in the panelling. Goes every so often into commerce until commerce fails every time. Night thins out and the dark can drain away out of the corridors. And mostly it does.

It's as if some sunny splendour has not long since passed through this room and the passage beyond with the power to lift the air and move, while the cartons and packing cases maintain an oppressive inertia bordering on menace.

Even though this long old box of a room – matt paintwork, scraps of brocade – is out of use it has been a small theatre and will be again: so it can never be empty or silent. A crackle of static. Ach, not *again* already.

Provision stretched and strained almost to snapping point. The note still dull.

Can it be nature's way that the first cottage in the terrace should have no back? A two-storey wagon-tilt of canvas bellying and sucking. By day, cooking and washing on the bare earth. At night fireworks start up from across the street outside the only bedroom with a window.

Rattle a Cart

Horse or dog or wolf or nag
broken from a flapping track

somewhere north: the judges' cabin
lopsided, minus windows, mysterious

only till walked through for a minute;
palings gapped, flattened and wet

on the grown-out turf. Kick one,
the nettles show white.

Peeling the present off the past
the better to show the wiring

through soot-flecked lines of washing
horse comes loping like a dog

spat on by losers, *ya great jallywow!*
rattling a cart of knocked-up planks

its bottom littered with research papers
on land use in the Fertile Crescent,

pamphlets, a Herodotus:
news of the stolen world.

NOTES

I am indebted to Joe Fisher for the title of this book, his coinage for the plain way of talking we people of central England like to believe we have.

Hole, Horse and Hellbox

Born in South America and having at first no knowledge of his ancestry in England, the artist, printer and publisher Ronald King learned only when his own career was well-established that seven generations of the male line had been laying down a prehistory for his chosen activities. Many of the consequent discoveries and some objects went into the making of his 'Tabernacle', an intricate artwork in the form of a cabinet. My sequence of poems, the title incorporating printers' slang for various stages of a print job, evoke the progress of the generations through three centuries.

Selected bibliography

POETRY BOOKS BY ROY FISHER

City (Migrant Press, 1961)
Ten Interiors with Various Figures (Tarasque Press, 1966)
The Ship's Orchestra (Fulcrum Press, 1966)
Collected Poems (Fulcrum Press, 1968)
Matrix (Fulcrum Press, 1971)
The Cut Pages (Fulcrum Press, 1971; Shearsman, 1986)
The Thing About Joe Sullivan: Poems 1971-1977 (Carcanet, 1978)
Poems 1955-1980 (Oxford University Press, 1980)
A Furnace (Oxford University Press, 1986)
Poems 1955-1987 (Oxford University Press, 1988)
Birmingham River (Oxford University Press, 1994)
It Follows That (Pig Press, 1994)
The Dow Low Drop: New & Selected Poems (Bloodaxe Books, 1996)
The Long & the Short of It: Poems 1955-2005 (Bloodaxe Books, 2005)
Standard Midland (Bloodaxe Books, 2010)

ESSAYS / INTERVIEWS / PROSE / OTHER

Roy Fisher: *Nineteen Poems and an Interview* (Grosseteste, 1975)
Robert Sheppard & Peter Robinson: *News for the Ear:
a homage to Roy Fisher* (Stride Publications, 2000)
Tony Frazer (ed.): *Interviews Through Time and Selected Prose*
(Shearsman Books, 2000)
Peter Robinson & John Kerrigan (eds.): *The Thing About Roy Fisher:
Critical Essays on the Poetry of Roy Fisher*
(Liverpool University Press, 2000)
Peter Robinson (ed.): *An Unofficial Roy Fisher* (Shearsman, 2010)